Confusing Mind
Confusing Time

Confusing Mind Confusing Time

Adrian Hamilton

Published by Adrian Hamilton, 2022.

Author: Adrian Hamilton

ACKNOWLEDGEMENT

Thanks to everyone's encouragement. I am continuing to write this book, special thanks to my best friend Jerry Lezama (deceased) for giving me the inspiration making sure I complete the book.

A special thanks to the gentleman who told me, whatever I put my mind to, I can accomplish anything. I thank the Home for the Aged, and the caregivers for talking to me.

The gentleman I connected with, who gave me his blessings to write about his ordeal between father and daughter.

ABOUT THIS BOOK

The book is based on a true story, an Elderly Gentleman I had the pleasure and privilege of meeting while on my vacation. It is about the Elderly Gentleman and his daughter; she placing him in a Home for the Elderly.

His anger and hatred for his daughter was very intense, mentioning her name got him furious. He was positive that his stay at the home was for the rest of his life, put there and held against his wishes.

With the negativity against his daughter, returned to his home after the renovations and liked what they did to the house.

Hi! Tom, where are you going this time on your travels? Billy asked.

I am going to my country of origin Grenada, in the Caribbean, also known as the Isle of Spice, where I was born. I still have family there.

What are you going to do when you get there?

Don't really know as yet, one thing that I have to do is visit all my family and people I know.

How long are you going away for, and are you staying with family?

I don't think so; I like the freedom of doing things when I want to without family; Do things their way.

Where would you be staying?

At a friend's place, I know about the countryside. I told him I was coming, and he said, I can stay there. The last time I was there, I helped him set up a Protocol Binder of rules for his business he was opening. A Home for the Elderly.

So; you are staying at an elderly home.

Yes, it's not what you may think. I will have my room, and everything I need, and it's on a bus route with easy access to transportation.

The day came that I was starting my vacation. I packed everything with the things that I was taking with me on my trip. I left for the airport early that day. The sun was still shining brightly on that cold winter day.

The forecast for that evening I was leaving said snow all night, and well into the next day, stopping around noon. I was glad that I had chosen a great day to leave.

A wonderful friend drove me to the airport, and after saying goodbye, I checked in at the airline counter, cleared customs, and had a seat waiting to board the plane. After an hour, they announced passengers should start boarding the plane; it did not take long for all passengers to board.

It delayed us for about fifteen minutes because the plane had to be de-iced on the runway before taking off. After deicing, we took off, and as it got up into the air, I thanked "GOD" softly for our safe arrival and on time. After six hours in the air, the pilot announced we should land soon, giving us the temperature and the weather for the day.

The landing could not have been any better, it was one of the gentlest touch down I have ever witnessed in all my travels; the plane taxied to the terminal gate, embarking from the plane, everyone proceeded to the immigration and customs area to have their passport stamped and verified.

I checked out of customs in less than twenty minutes, proceeded to the exit door of the terminal, made a call to the home where I was going to stay, to make sure my friend was home. They were no answer, so I ended the call, and he had no answering system.

The airport had with lots of amenities. I had breakfast and took a mini-bus to the capital of the island St. Georges, which took about twenty minutes. I took another mini-bus to another town passing through the mountains, just enjoying the greenery of the vegetation and the colorful houses dotted amongst the trees and along the roadside.

Breathing was much healthier because of the fresh air than what I was used to. I could not be more at peace, and driven by a competent driver who was very careful around every corner, and every turn going up and down through the mountains.

What is so spectacular was the scenery, and the magnificent greenery, with such deep green and luscious vegetation along the roadside, at every turn not forgetting the breath-taking views of the distance hills where houses were wondering to yourself, how did they get up there to build these houses, and planning the colors that enhanced the mountainside.

After arriving in another town, which took about forty-five minutes, I took another mini-bus to my final destination, about fifteen minutes' drive, walked up a little hill where the house was located and where I was going to be staying. I announced my arrival, and greeted by my friend James, the owner of The Home for the Elderly.

He took me to my sleeping quarters and the facilities area where I would perform my daily activities. James left because he had some errands to complete, but said that he will catch up later and talk about all that was happening when last I saw him.

After setting my suitcase in my quarters, I made my way upstairs of the house to relax, while enjoying the view of the coastal layout, and the cool, calming breeze coming off the ocean. The breeze was constantly blowing, and because of it, I got sleepy. Suddenly I heard the tapping on the floor of the living room, out came an elderly gentleman, who was staying at the home.

Hello he said,

Hello I replied, watching me from head to toe.

Who are you, and where did you come from?

I hesitated to give him an answer, but gave him a short version that he seems ok with, but continued watching me suspiciously as if to say "I don't trust you."

I made him feel at ease by telling him my name, Thomas Greaves, born in the town just down from here. His eyes opened wide with an astonishing look.

He said, I know some of your relatives they lived in the same village where I grew up.

He still did not tell me his name, maybe he was not sure what to think of me, that was understandable because he was seeing me for the first time, as the saying goes first time impression is very good, when you are meeting anyone for the first time.

Although we exchanged a few words, I could see that he was more relaxed than before, just because he was seeing me for the first time. It was hard for him to talk to a stranger he had just met.

He said, as we looked towards the ocean, I would sure like to go down to the beach one day.

You mean, you have not gone to the beach.

No, I have not he replied, James does not have the time to take me, he kept saying one of these days.

I am sure he meant it.

Let's talk about the weather he said, do you think it will rain.?

I don't think so, it's too sunny for rain I said.

But there is a possibility it could, someday it's very sunny and without notice we can get a heavy downpour.

Observing the whitecaps on the water in the distance as the waves formed, and the breeze blew, the day was looking as though it will be a hot one, but that constant breeze off the ocean was cool enough for being enjoyed.

The trees were swaying back and forth, and the cooling effects of the breeze had me nodding off. The elderly gentleman whose name I do not know as yet began muttering words I could not understand, as though he was angry about something.

Please excuse me for a while. I need to get some rest but I will be back I said.

Okay; he said I will sit here; it will be soon for my tea bread.

He watched me walk down the steps into the downstairs living room entrance. After two hours' rest I returned upstairs, but he was not sitting on the verandah.

Hi; are you there I said?

I am inside he shouted back; I don't feel like talking anymore for the day.

Okay, it's your choice. Whenever you feel up to it, let me know.

I remained upstairs and relaxed, enjoying the sea breeze that blew towards the home. They were no activity inside from the gentleman I met today. It was now 6:30 pm and dark so; I walked down the steps, got something to eat, had a shower and the moment my head rest on the pillow, I fell asleep, and was out like a light.

During the night I heard the shifting of furniture's, coming from above my room, although the gentleman's room whose name I do not know as yet; slept in a corner room. It did not sound as though it was coming from his room.

After getting accustom to the noise that night, I fell asleep, got up very early in the morning and took a walk through the neighborhood. I took a shower after my walk being sweaty because of the heat of the sun, had breakfast and proceeded upstairs to continue my conversation with the elderly gentleman, before reaching the top of the stairs.

Hi, the voice of the elderly gentleman called out.

Good morning to you, I replied.

He was watching me, walked up the steps, and waited until I was in full view of him.

Good morning, he said, how was your sleep?

Very well, thank you was my reply. The only thing that kept me awake for a while was some shifting of furniture.

He watched me, and with a funny smile, looked at me, then said.

The noise was coming from my room.

Why I asked? Were you moving furniture during the night?

He had a small grin on his face, and said, to block the door so no one can enter to do me any harm.

You know, that is a safety issue.

I don't really care; was the reply he gave me.

What do you think about today's weather rain or no rain?

I don't really care whether it rains.

Seems to me you like mangoes, I said in a friendly voice.

You bet, he said; I can eat mangoes all day instead of breakfast.

Tell me a little about yourself. Who are you? And where did you come; from your accent you sound thought it is British.

Only if you tell me about yourself first he said.

Okay, I agreed to tell him about myself, that I was born on the Island, and where I lived before moving abroad.

Hold it there for a moment. Let me tell you a little about myself. I left the Island at seventeen, a couple days after a major hurricane, had ravaged the island. I left for England along with James's brother. When I got to England, I knew no one there and had to fend for myself, stayed with James' brother John for a while.

A couple days after I began my job hunting, it was hard at first but I had no other choice; it was I starve or eat, so I ate. I found a job just in time because the money I had was slowly dwindling. I remember starting the job on a Monday morning at 7:00 am at H. J Heinz in Manchester.

He opened up talking more and eventually told me his name. Wow!

I prefer to use my initials, J.W. S he said.

What does J.W. S stand for?

My full name is James Winston Simon, he said.

Is it okay for me to call you Sio?

Yes, he replied, I like the sound of Sio.

My first and only job was working with the tomato ketchup giant Heinz until I reached the age of retirement.

Let me describe who Sio is and what exactly he is all about. He is an average gentleman, in his early eighties, but looks like he is nineties years of age. His hair is black and gray (salt and pepper) walks with a limp, has a smirky grin, and a cantankerous laugh, and can be serious. His eyes are brown, and stands five feet nine inches tall, weighs around one hundred and ninety pounds.

My priority after getting a job was to bring my mother up to England to live with me after I settled down. It took a couple of years, but before doing that, I had to see about buying a flat.

Are you a proud man I asked?

You can say that I am proud of the things that I have done for my mother. After all, she made that sacrifice to get me to England.

Although he looks older than eighty, he has his wits about him. He would just start laughing.

What are you laughing about now?

I remember as a young man, living on the street in a mixed neighborhood, the flogging I got one night, from a group of boys called the Teddy Boys gang.

How bad was the flogging I asked?

Let me tell you he said, I could not sit on a hard chair for two days. I had to sit on something soft. Does that answer your question?

Yes! it did, I said. He looked at me and smile.

I had to endure all those hardships because of who I was, and what I was he said.

I got married in my thirties to a beautiful woman; we had three children, a girl and two boys.

Where did you meet your wife?

Oh! In England, she was also from this island. We gave the children the best education possible.

What school did you attend on the Island?

I went to school in the country, not in the city. I walked to school, could not afford it. My mother was a single parent.

Would you say that you a highly educated?

No; but I have a vast knowledge of many things.

What did you do when you were not working?

I repair autos in my spare time. I would visit the junk yard and buy damage autos, fix them up and sell them for a little profit.

What was your favorite auto?

The Volvo, because of its durability. I would buy a couple and park them in the driveway, dismantle them, and sell the parts sometimes.

Was there a demand for the parts?

Oh yes! I would sell the whole auto, if someone wants it for parts.

He was brilliant in his thinking, and what he said all in a British accent, and sometimes uses phrases he had learned as a boy, growing up on the island of his birth.

Are you proud of your heritage?

Most definitely, I would have it no other way he replied.

Let's change the topic and let me tell you about my children and their names.

My daughter's name is Theresa (Resa) and my son's names are Andrew (Andy) and Kenneth (Kenny) he said, but I dislike calling my daughter by her name.

Why is that, I ask?

My daughter has caused me so much pain, and heartache, while growing up, he said.

I wish she was not my daughter, because of the bad things she used to do.

What kind of daughter causes a father so much pain?

I don't really know, "I said. " I cannot answer that question.

After I had done for her while growing up, giving her the best of everything I could, he said.

It was very disturbing to hear him talked about her, with so much anger in his voice, as he talked, clenching his fist, and waving in the air.

If she was here, and came near me, I would cuff her to the ground he said.

What year did you retire and return to the island?

If my memory serves me right, I think I retired in two thousand, and returned in two thousand and five.

Since returning to the island, what have you been doing?

Nothing really; just a little backyard gardening.

Do you have any other names besides Sio that other people call you?

"Sure" by my closest friends, the money man.

Why is that, if I may ask?

People think I have lots of money because of my big house, and with all the amenities available to me, and is on a hill next to the golf course.

Do you have lots of money?

That is not, so he said, what people's opinion is of me is not true, but I let them think that I have lots of money.

My question to you is:

Stop right there he said, let me say this, my daughter is living on the island. I have done lots for her although she treated me badly, but I helped her build an addition to her house.

Do you have any regrets helping her, although she mistreated you?

Yes; I do have regrets but, what done is done, I do not want to get into details about it?

Okay, I replied.

Let me tell you about my second son, Kenny. He is tall, about six feet, light brown in complexion, has short hair, and is a very handsome person.

Are you proud of him?

Yes! But he has lots of women, and so many children, that I cannot keep track of the names of my grandchildren.

How many children does Kenny have? Do you know them by name?

Yes, but at my age, I can only remember the first three of his children.

Anyone of them is your favorite.

Yes! I love them all, but the one he named after himself, Kenny Jr. is special to me.

Why is he so special to you?

He lived with me for a couple of years at my home before coming to this elderly home managed by James.

So; how did you come to live at the home here?

That is another day's discussion, he said, but right now, no more questions.

He had a smirk on his face, and a cynical laugh, put his hands together, pointing his fingers towards heaven.

That's it for today, he said, no more talk. I am going to my room.

Today is another day of my vacation. I am still hopeful Sio will talk to me about how he came to live in the home where he is. I walked out of the downstairs living room, and into the yard, looking for any mangoes that fell overnight, then a familiar voice hailed out to me in a friendly manner.

Good morning;

Yes, it's a wonderful morning. The sun was just rising, and the sky is, blue, I said.

Are there any mangoes on the ground as he waved at me? If so, can I get at least a couple he asked?

Sure, you can get a couple. How about six would that be okay with you? I said.

That would be great, he answered back.

Okay, let me wash them, and I will bring them up to you.

Thank you very much, he said; I may not cross the gate by myself, otherwise I would have gone looking for mangoes myself.

That's no problems, glad I can be of help to you.

On any day, he said, I would eat about six mangoes, half of a pawpaw, and two bananas.

That's a lot of fruits for one man I said.

Yes, I know, but I love mangoes, especially the sweet ones they call Julie mangoes.

It was really a beautiful morning; the sun was just above the ocean floor, and the cool breeze was blowing towards the house. The weatherman predictions for the day, was it is going to a scorcher, another day with temperature in the high range of thirty degrees Celsius plus, but because of the constant breeze coming off the ocean, it would have no effect on us.

Are we going to continue our conversation where we left off yesterday?

We sure will, after I have completed my morning routine, around eight o'clock give and take a few minutes he said.

Sio, his caregiver, said, it's time for your bath, shave and to change your clothes.

His caregiver at the home was very pleasant, consistent, and patient with him. Her name was Margaret, short in stature, about four feet nine inches, heavy, about one hundred and forty pounds, black hair, and spoke in a soft voice. She lived close to the home about ten minutes' walk.

Don't feel like doing any of my morning routine today he said to her.

Sio was being sort of cantankerous, putting up a strong resistance, showing Margaret who rules, but that is who he is.

Sio, I said, let's have a little chat, you know, that it is very healthy that you do your morning routine every morning.

Yes, he replied, but..........

No buts, just go and get it done, so we can talk.

Okay, he called out to Margaret, saying; I am ready to have my bath.

An hour had gone by since Sio went to do his morning routine, returning to the verandah smelling nice, looking fresh and all cleaned up. He looked like a brand new man, as if he was going on a date.

I am ready for my breakfast he said to Margaret.

Before sitting down to eat, looked out at the ocean, and enjoyed the view, then began to eat eggs, bacon, and toast with a cup of hot cocoa.

Do you know where I would like to go today?

Where would that be? I said?

To the beach and have a swim he replied.

You know, I cannot take you unless James tells me it's okay; but you know, it would not be possible.

I will say nothing to him. If you take me, he replied.

It is not my responsibility; They trust you to James while at the home.

Well; okay, I was just trying to see if you will go along with the idea.

Nice try;

You know, "we are like two fish in a kettle," he said.

What does that mean, explain that saying to me?

It means that we are of the same color, but different parentage, and have unique knowledge of things, was his answer.

Okay, I can see where you are going with this. That makes sense.

I get angry with myself, whenever I think, and ask, why did I return to the Island?

Do you have an answer to that question I asked him?

No! not really, I left a lot of things in England, maybe it would have been better if I had stayed there.

Why do you think that?

I don't want to talk about that right now, memories.

So; why did you leave England? And return to the island you left years ago.

Because this is home to me, the Island is where my heritage started, my house that I built is here.

Did you enjoy living in England?

Oh yes! He replied; I loved working at the Heinz Company. I had many friends and traveled to different places in England.

Have you traveled to any other place?

Sure, I took a ferry to France for the first; the sea was rough, and scary, but I opened my eyes to the beauty of the land on the other side of England.

Did you enjoy France while you were there?

You bet I did; I must leave you. I feel like taking a nap now.

Okay, then I will see you after your nap.

He left and went into his room, while I stayed upstairs enjoying the scenery of the white caps of the waves on the ocean as they rolled onto the shore. I began thinking to myself, why did Sio, come back to live, and id now living at the elderly home, is it because he could no longer live on his own, or was there another reason, that I would definitely like to know.

I made my way downstairs after twenty minutes, went to my room, and had a nap, still thinking to myself, what made him returned to the Island, since he told me that England was where he wanted to be, and where he would have been better off, in terms of medical help.

Although he told me he was in a good place, he wished he could get on a plane back to England. Why go back to England? If you have no one close to your age, you could talk to during the day, much more talk with someone about your problems.

As I lay relaxing on the bed before getting up, I heard the tapping of his cane, which he uses sometimes to balance himself, while walking back and forth. Although he can walk sometimes on his own without it, he has to use the cane, because he is unstable on his feet, but tries not to use it from time to time.

The tapping continued all the way into the verandah, until they were a silent pause, and I know he had positioned himself in his usual seat. Ding a ling, ding a ling when his bell to summons his caregiver.

He shouted to Margaret, I will like to have my tea, and toast with peanut butter please.

It was about three- fifteen the time he has his tea, living in England, all these years he gained the British habit of being a tea drinker. I made my way upstairs just around four o'clock, while sipping his tea and eating his toast and peanut butter, continued talking not about anything of interest, just small talk.

Do you have any information, what the weather is for tomorrow, rain or hot again as today?

I do not know, have not listened to the radio, but the weather can change during the night, and early morning.

I am a very patience man at times, but can be easily riled up, when provoked he said.

Is that so; what would it take to get you riled up? I asked.

Ha-ha, you don't want to know, and I hope you never see it he replied.

One thing about Sio, he tells it like it is, without holding and punches back, which I observed the third day I was here. The sun was setting over the coconut trees, and a gentle breeze had the branches fluttering. Sio was having a late supper, which was unusual for him, after having his tea, toast and a couple of mangoes. I guess he was not hungry. After he had finished eating, he got up.

All that sea breeze has me sleepy. I am going to say good night and left.

I watched him as he made his way towards his room, tapping on the floor, until they were no more tapping, slammed his door, making sure he shut it for the night. They did not involve James with his daily itinerary, but Margaret was in charge of that. Anything that she thinks she needed for Sio, she got the okay from James to get the items.

I still have not seen James, because he was busy, gone in the mornings when I get up, but left a note saying that soon we will sit down, and talk. After a good night's sleep, I got up early in the morning and went for a long walk. Sio was not on the verandah when I left, but I can see Sio's head when I returned from my walk.

Hello, my boy; how was your morning walk?

Very good, I replied.

Could you check to see if they are any mangoes on the ground, he shouted.

Let me look and see; yes! Only three this morning.

There was a big smile on his face. He said okay.

I am going to wash them first. How many do you want?

Two will be good, thank you.

Then two it is; I said.

Thank you, my boy; he said as I handed him the mangoes.

You are most welcome!

They sure smell good. Now let's see how sweet this one is, um! Now this is sweet.

The juice trickling down the side of your mouth licked his lips and wipe the juice off.

Now, that's how sweet a mango should be, he said.

Is it to your satisfaction I asked?

Yes! And more, he replied, as he bit into the second one.

Are you going to have breakfast after eating these mangoes?

Oh yes, as soon as it gets here.

Okay, then I will see you after my shower and breakfast.

Sure, I am looking forward to the visit.

I returned upstairs after my shower, and breakfast Sio was facing the ocean looking at the waves that was forming on the ocean, the breeze was cool, and one could fall asleep easily while sitting, and relaxing he turned around when he heard my footsteps, and continued our conversation.

Sio, how did you come to live in the home that you are presently living in?

I visited the home frequently when they had an open house. My daughter asked me on those occasions to visit it with her.

Why did you?

Just for the drive, and to see what the home was all about. I thought nothing of it, because I have my home.

At the time you visited, did you think that you would be living here?

Not on your life, my boy, he said in an angry voice.

Are you angry about being put here?

Yes! He said.

As the tears ran down his cheeks, and with clenched teeth together, looked towards Heaven, not saying a word but sobbing. I could see the pain and hurt on his face, the clenched teeth. It told me he was furious. He never spoke to me about it that day.

Whatever caused him all that hurt and pain, I hoped that someday he will tell me about it. Today is not that day. It took several minutes for his pain, anger, and hurt to subside, and we began talking once again.

At the time of the home open house, did you like the quiet surroundings?

Yes! My good boy, I thought nothing of it, and gave it no thought that anything was being planned behind my back each time I came for a visit.

Now, did you think living here was planned by your daughter?

I would have to say a big yes! Okay, let's change the subject. Do you have any plans for today?

Yes, I said; I am going into town for a while after lunch. Do you need me to get you something?

No! I wish I could go with you, but walking will be difficult for me he said.

Sio, get ready for your bath and shave, Margaret said from downstairs.

Excuse me, my boy, he said, after putting up a fuss.

Come now, Margaret said, as she followed him to the bathroom.

He was away for a long time, but; it was just about twenty minutes; he emerged looking very smart, well dressed, and shaven with a big smile on his face from ear to ear.

You know what, my boy; I love to create havoc, just to see Margaret's face, and her reaction. I know she is not happy with my attitude.

Margaret brought his breakfast, placed it on a table, but he just picked at it. After eating two big mangoes earlier, he was not hungry. He drank his tea while talking, nothing constructive, just repeating most of the things he had already told me.

I enjoy repeating things; he said. It gives me confidence to hold a conversation, bringing me closer to remembering where my conversation stopped.

I gave him a prompt where we had left off.

Oh yes; I remember now.

Then the tears started running down his cheeks. After wiping his tears, he continued talking. He would always say these words to me before he talks.

My boy! My house sits on a hill next to a golf course, and I have all the necessities that I want.

Your house that you describe to me. How big is it in the sense of bedrooms?

There are three bedrooms, and bathrooms in each. I worked very hard to build my home, and I am happy with it.

Any regrets about the way things turned out?

Yes! My only regret is that I did not return to live on the island after retiring, but remained in England for a couple more tears.

Why did you remain in England after retiring?

At the time I had a girlfriend, who had a child for me, she lived not too far from me in England, later on in our relationship, she moved to Canada to live, with her son, so she left a couple months after mentioning it.

Did you wish, somehow, you could have made her change her mind about moving to Canada?

Sometimes, I think about it. I should have asked her to marry me, after my wife died, just did not get around to ask her.

Why not? Did you have cold feet asking her to marry you?

No! I was too busy doing other things, and asking her to marry me was not on the top of my list. Wish I had made it a priority.

Sio had a sad look on his face, while he talked about his regrets, and the look said it all, as though it was a big mistake, he had now come to regret over the past couple of years.

Anyway, mistakes I forget, and I lived with and move on, he said.

Do you get to talk to her, while you are here at the home?

Sure, (with a great big smile on his face) she calls once a week on Sundays after supper. We talk for an hour or so, but I feel sad when she has to say goodbye.

What about her son? Does he call you?

Yep! You mean my son. Whom I have with her, he calls me on a regular basis.

What do you talk about anything in particular?

Just about anything, he told me that he would like to live on the Island, but his mother wants him close to her.

What is her name, if I may ask?

Well! My boy, that is for me to know, and you to find out, and I will not give you her name.

Do you blame her for keeping him away from seeing you?

No; because it's her only child that I can understand. I do not want him to live here, but he can visit anytime he wishes, and by the way, my other children do not know that they have a half-brother.

When was the last time you saw him?

I have not seen him in twelve years; he said. My heart breaks. Whenever he speaks to me, tears flow from my eyes just hearing his voice.

Is it hard on you not seeing your son in the last twelve years?

Definitely, living without seeing him is very hard. I my old age I would love to see him before passing on he replied.

Do you think you will ever see him again?

Who knows, my boy; I hope someday he would surprise me with a visit.

You would like to see that happen, won't you?

Sure will; okay let's change the topic.

Okay I said, what will you like to talk about today?

Today, I wish I can go to see some place I have never been before he replied.

In my mind, I know where he will rather be right now, at his home in the city. Then he looked at me and said.

Stop! Let's talk again tomorrow.

Before leaving Margaret, brought him his supper, returning to my room I put on my sneakers, and went for a walk before it got dark, on the Island as soon as the sun goes down between five-forty-five, and six o'clock it gets dark.

Today marks the first week of my stay at the home and on the island, and I have not seen James, to have a chat with him. The morning sun came out over the ocean horizon, but gave way to a cloudy sky, and looking at the horizon, you can actually see the rain approaching.

Being blown by the wind's force, spraying the home with a heavy downpour of water hitting the side of the house, and entering the verandah. The rain was very heavy, and I have not seen rain drops that big in a very long time.

The sound it made on the galvanize roof gave me a sense of being in a storm, reminding me when I was younger that when it is raining the best thing to do is get under the sheets and cover up. The heavy pounding of the raindrops on the roof was something everyone at the home was accustom of hearing.

No one came out onto the verandah because of the water. And also the chairs were wet. The rain fell hard and sounded violent. The trees were swaying back and forth as the wind blew; it was not an enjoyable morning for anyone to be caught in the rain.

The heavy downpour caused the drains to be filled with water, and you could see the swiftness of the water as it came through the drains, overflowing unto the street. As the vehicles pass, you could see the splashing from the tires as they drive through the water.

After an hour of heavy rain, it finally subsided, but the drizzle continued. In the sky beyond the horizon, a rainbow formed, as though it touched the sea, showing off its magnificent colors as a proud peacock. The drizzle stopped, and the sun came out with such a passionate fury, as though you were heating an oven.

It took a while for the verandah to dry off, and Sio could return to his usual spot, he sat every day. The tapping of his walking stick could was heard, and I knew he was on his way out to sit on the verandah. I returned upstairs to continue our conversation, but he was not willing to continue at the moment.

My boy, he said, that was some heavy rain, and wind we just experienced.

Isn't is, I have not experienced that hard a downpour in many years?

Sio did not want to talk about anything of interest. I excused myself for a bit and took a short walk to the grocery store to buy a couple of bottles of drinks to cool myself down. My phone rang as I was paying for my groceries and reached for it.

Hello; I said a voice I have not heard for a while, a Reverend friend of my who I met a long time ago when I visited the Island before.

What are you doing later, she asked?

Nothing of importance. Why? I replied.

I will pick you up. Can you be ready by five thirty? I want to show you a piece of land that I want to build a church on.

Okay, I will be ready, and waiting at the entrance around five thirty.

Bye, see you then, hand up.

Returning home from the grocery store, I took a shower, dressed, and walked down to the entrance of the driveway. I was told to be ready, and within five minutes of standing at the entrance, she pulled up. I got into the car; she introduced to me her daughter who was driving.

She was visiting her mother for two weeks from America. We arrived at the site after a five minutes' drive. She introduced me to all her parishioners, that were present, looked at the site where she was planning to build the church, and gave her my views on how I perceived the building will look on the land.

It was getting dark, but she had another surprise. She mentioned she was having a prayer meeting and asked if I could stay, which I did. The land where the church was going to be built was close to where I was staying. It was within walking distance.

I would say about twenty minutes' walk, which was an excellent exercise for me, in the morning before the sun gets hot. I arrived home around ten o'clock that night, after viewing the site, staying for a prayer meeting, and Bible study. I did my nightly routine, and off to bed for a good night's sleep, hoping for a pleasant conversation with Sio in the morning.

The neighbor's rooster woke me up early with its loud crowing, and also the dog in the house's front began barking. It was warning us that someone was coming up the driveway or passing in front of the entrance.

I did my morning routine, had breakfast, and waited to hear for any movement of the tapping of Sio's walking stick, but unfortunately not a sound. I came to the conclusion he was still in his bedroom sleeping. I relaxed for a while, then made my way outside to look for any mangoes that may have fallen overnight, as I was starting to gather the mangoes. A voice came out from now where.

Good morning my boy, the can I have a couple of those mangoes please.

Sure I replied, but I thought you were still sleeping.

No; got up early to see when you were coming outside to look for mangoes.

You seem to be in a better mood today I said.

Yes, he shouts back.

So; we are going to talk some more today about some of your problems.

Yes! He said in a low voice.

I will bring some up to you in a bit, okay.

Well my boy, he said, how many mangoes did you collect today?

About eight this morning, and gave him five to eat before or after his breakfast.

Hey, Margaret, he shouted, I am going to skip breakfast but have only tea.

Okay she replied, I will bring it up soon.

Sio bit into the first mango, and all I heard him say was, Um! This is delicious.

He sank his teeth into the second and third mangoes before having his tea.

I am full. I could not eat another thing right now he said.

Did I just hear you say you are full?

Yes, my boy, you heard right.

Sio fell asleep after drinking his tea, as the gentle breeze blew towards the house from off the ocean. I left him to catch a couple minutes of shut eyes, returned to my room until he called out to me. It was close to one o'clock before I heard his voice again.

Oh; Margaret, I am hungry. I would like toast with peanut butter, and a cup of tea please, he said.

This was one of his favorite things he liked to eat, regardless of the time of day. It was well into the late afternoon we got talking again, so I listened while he speaks.

The gentleman here, I think he, and my daughter are having an affair.

You mean James? How do you know that? I asked.

Well! I heard him talking on the phone about going to see her.

Are you sure that it what you heard? It could have been any person.

"Yes, I am sure"

Could it be, what you heard was something all entirely different from what you think you heard.

No! I heard what I heard, and that is that.

I will not argue with you. If you say that is what you heard, so be it I said.

As soon as Sio said these words to me, James came outside to talk with both of us, but Sio went after him with his walking stick, and immediately taken away from him, because he attacked James

You are a son of a bitch, a liar, and a womanizer. "I will kill you," Sio shouted.

Sio carried on ranting and raving for quite a very long time, before calming down, got up without saying a word, and went into his room. My thoughts were that Sio was mad at himself for acting the way he did. I am not sure why he attacked James, but they had to be a good reason for him to do so, other than what he overheard.

I really thought today of all days that Sio will tell me more about how he came to be living in the elderly home. I do not know how long it will take him to calm down and get his composure together. I got a glimpse of Sio's anger, and expressions on his face along with the clenching fist, and the many adjectives he used to describe James.

Night was slowly creeping in, and as the sun set, it gave up the light to the darkness, but rising on the horizon towards the ocean was the moon, which came up very fast, and before long showed off its illumination in the sky along with the many stars.

Yes, another beautiful day has arrived, and Sio was sitting on the verandah waiting for me to visit him when he heard me talking to Margaret before he called out.

Good morning my boy; are you going to look for any mangoes that may have fallen during the night?

Not really, but I will take a quick look around.

Have you found any as yet, he shouted?

Yes; I did, only four. I will wash them and give you two.

Thank you my boy, I will eat them later, during the day.

Sio did not have breakfast as ye, it was still a bit early for him, but had a cup of tea, prior to having breakfast, Margaret brought his breakfast brought his breakfast to him around eight o'clock he looked at it, for a while before eating, this morning he was having something on the island we call fish cakes, with sliced tomatoes.

Sio, Margaret said, after breakfast, get ready for your shower.

You know, I hate showering this early. Can I take it later?

No! Margaret said, right after breakfast, go into the bathroom. I will have it ready, and you will come up to see you.

Ah! Okay, he replied.

I will come back and see you I said, and we can continue our conversation.

Agreed, he said.

Hello; my boy he shouted from the verandah, are you coming up?

Yes; in a couple minutes, I shouted back.

Okay, take your time.

Now there is a well-dressed man, all groomed, hair combed, shaven, and in clean clothes, I said.

Well, thank you, my boy.

Are you ready to continue our conversation I asked?

Okay, let's make a go at it, and see how far we will get today.

What is the reason that you think James is having an affair with your daughter?

"Well! He said. " I just know he is. In the first place, he encouraged her to send me here to live, although I have my house. I had a caregiver, Mrs. Green. I lived close to the shopping mall and bank.

Were you in control doing things your way, with no difficulty?

Sometimes he replies, for instance, I control my money myself with no help, but I would forget I had a pot on the stove, not that I am forgetful, but did not remember. I thought I had turned off the stove.

Don't you think that is a bit much? Leaving the stove on with a pot on the fire, I replied.

Sometimes, but I did not do it all the time he fired back.

How did you come to in the home?

My daughter came to visit me frequently at my house, and up to that time we had a good relationship. He said.

What happened the day she visited you?

Dad; the house needs repairs. Do you remember the place where we went to open house twice? she said.

Yes! I replied.

Well! How about you staying there for a while until they completed the repairs, and then you can have returned to the house?

I told her okay, she had some papers she wanted me to sign.

Did you sign the papers?

Yes! I did because I trusted her, so without reading to see what was on the paper, I signed, figuring I was only giving her permission to go ahead with the repairs the house needed.

What happened after you signed the papers?

I did not know. I was giving her ownership of the house, along with managing my finances, leaving me with no chance of having control of my assets.

How did you feel after; you had read the papers?

Furious, tell me my friend, how will you feel if your daughter duped you into thinking she was looking after your best interest?

I will get angry, I said. Maybe she thought it was the better for you.

I don't know if she had any motive for doing what she did to me.

Why do you think that?

I have no money in my possession, and cannot buy or go anywhere if I want.

Does that bother you a lot? Not having money in your possession, I asked?

Yes! Sure it does. That is one reason that is frustrating and gets me angry. Whenever I talk to her, it is a complete screaming match between us.

Do you feel as though she has totally abandoned you?

Sometimes I think so; after all I had done for her with my money.

What things have you done for her, I asked?

I gave her money to put an addition on her house. No questions asked, he said?

Have you had any visits or phone calls from her, after she placed you at the home.

No! none, no calls, or visits because she knows, if she does what may happen, he said.

The tears began flowing. With both his fist and jaw clenched, the anger in him took charge. I waited a while for his anger to subside, not saying anything to him, but thinking to myself what I was going to say to him, but could not find the word.

I would be angry with myself if my daughter duped me the way she did him. After about an hour, give and take, he smiled and started muttering words. I could not understand what he was saying. Soon after, he began speaking again.

I have so much hatred for my daughter; he said.

Why do you have so much hatred for your daughter, I asked him?

Because of the way she treated me, then and presently he replied.

Are you ever going to see her?

No! not now, and maybe never, if ever she comes to visit I don't know what I will do to her.

Is it that bad between you two?

Yes! And what makes it worst, James is preventing me from going anywhere.

He was talking about James when he passed by, and Sio actually abuse him with words, calling him every name in the book that describes him, and some that I have never heard by anyone that I know when they are angry.

Sometimes I feel like walking away from here, and go anywhere but I am unstable on my feet, and no money in my pocket, makes it useless to try, not only that I don't have a clue where I am going or what bus to take that would get me into town.

So what are you going to do? Now that you don't have any means of going into town.

Let's leave it at that, he said.

He sat, thinking and was silent for a while, with tears flowing down his cheeks and pointing up at the sky.

"God help me" if I get the chance to leave here, there is no way I will come back, he said.

Are you serious, wanting to leave the home?

Yes, I really do; I need to get out of here and will do anything to leave.

I felt sorry for Sio, knowing that I could not take him anywhere, because he was not my responsibility. In fact, none of his family came to see him while I was there. The only person who called him was his girlfriend, and son who live in Canada. After talking to them, his face would light up.

I wish I was still living in England, instead of this Island, and this house where I cannot go anywhere, he said.

The reason you are not being taken out for a drive is because of the incident you had with James. Am I right!

Well! You have a point there, so what do I do now?

You need to calm down, to where James can see that you can be trusted in terms of your behavior.

In other words, you want mean I have to behave myself in a gentle and mannerly way.

Yes! You do I said, that's the only way James would take you to see the sights, or to the beach.

My boy, all I can do is try, but they are times that I cannot hold my tongue, most often when my daughter calls to say hello, and I get into a shouting fiasco, before she can get a word in.

If you try, and be calm while I am here for the next three weeks, I will ask James to take you out. Do you think you can manage to do that?

I am not going to say yes, directly; but I promise you, I will give it my best shot.

I am sure your daughter will love to visit you, but you are making it impossible for her to do so.

I love my daughter, don't get me wrong, but because she duped me into signing the papers, I remain angry, just hearing her voice or name mentioned.

Do you enjoy when other people visit you and sit talking with you?

Absolutely, I do; I feel at ease with them, but they cannot take me anywhere.

Why do you think so; I asked?

Because of my anger, they might not know what I may do while they are driving.

He cries very often, for nothing you can tell by his eyes. Although he does not bawl when he is crying, maybe it is because of being ashamed of letting anyone know he cries.

I like my tea, toast and peanut butter at the same time every day, he said; and sometimes I like to have a few crackers.

It's good to hear him talk about the way the British say the word a cup of tea. He can be gentle but can flip on a dime, cursing and swearing about what he can do to anyone that gets him angry. I have seen it happen.

I can sit and talk to you about anything you want to discuss he said, although I am not well educated, I will give you an argument on any topic, especially about cars and traveling.

I know, you are quite verse about cars. Have you traveled outside of England?

Oh yes! I took the ferry to France to do some shopping and sightseeing. I had such a great time, and visited there frequently after that.

Sio switched topics on me, and I had to think about what he was about to say to me, because his topics, and questioning, can be sometimes confusing, not only to me but to other people he is talking to. Not a word about his daughter, for a while today, which was good. His mood was relatively calm and exceptional, one he of his best days he had since I met him.

It was a good day, because he was not angry, and there was no reason for him to be. He would smile, giggle, or laugh out loud.

What are you laughing at now I asked?

A joke someone told me a long time ago, he replied?

Well; do you remember it?

Not that well, he said, but I will tell you, anyway.

It took me a while to understand the joke. When I couldn't, he explained what it meant.

In our conversations, he would talk to me about words his mother and grandmother said to him, while growing up, and now has passed it on down to his children, and what they all meant. Sio can be a handful. I remember one morning, while he was having breakfast.

Margaret said, Sio; you need to have a shower after eating your breakfast.

"Definitely not," he replied, back to her, not today.

Sio, I said, you need to have that shower before continuing our conversation.

Okay, he replied, it's not every time I feel like taking a shower.

Yes! I know how you feel, but because of your incontinent having a shower is mostly for your hygiene purpose.

Margaret, he shouted, I have finished my breakfast, and I am ready for my shower.

Okay! Margaret replied, see you in the bathroom in a couple minutes.

Looking at Sio, sometimes you can see a sinister smirk on his face. It's not an evil one, it is a look that he is giving you, saying, not today, you don't. if I have a conversation with him, I look at his face and watch his eyes as he talks to me. He may have something up his sleeves, but most of the times he is not conjuring any sinister thoughts.

How do you tell someone that is older than you that you have to take it easy? Especially if that person does not know how to relax, but constantly thinking how to get away from the elderly home thinking that he is *"HELD AGASINST HIS WISHES"*?

With all the phone calls that are being exchanged between his daughter, James and himself, He (Sio) alone knows how he is going to deal with the problem that is on his plate. Sio looked at me, as though he was dumb, but that is the way he looks sometimes, when he is thinking, what to do next, not there are any wicked thoughts, but how he may get someone to take him for a drive to his home in the city.

I waited and watched to see what his next move was going to be, but after waiting at least twenty minutes, nothing happened except nodding off to sleep, as the breeze kept blowing towards the house, which calmed him down. I left him sleeping, walked down the pathway onto the main road, and headed to the grocery store, returning to the house. A familiar voice called out to me.

Hello there, what have we got there?

A couple juice drinks I replied, do you want one?

Oh yes! Thank you he shouted.

He was standing, and holding on to the wall in the verandah, looking at me as I walked up the driveway. I put the drinks on the table downstairs and took one to him. His eyes lit up as though it was something out of the ordinary for him.

Thank you, my boy he said.

You are welcome anytime I replied.

How about politics I asked? What do you think about the political atmosphere that is having the country abuzz?

To tell you the truth, my boy; I am not into politics.

Just then, the phone rang. I handed it to him, without telling him who it was, the minute he said hello; and, he heard the voice on the other end of the phone, his facial expression changed immediately, and his pleasant mood he had before answering the phone changed to an unpleasant one instantly.

He did not give the person any chance to say much. He started calling the person, all the names he could think of, without swearing at them, and then slammed the phone down on the cradle, coming out to the verandah swearing.

I saw his facial expression as one that was disgusted, and his anger showing with his clenched fist. I knew it was his daughter; he did not have to say much, then his eyes sprang tears, looking up towards the sky, shook his head and buried his face in his hands.

After lifting his face from his hands, he looks me straight in the eyes, and I could see a bit of reflection, and the glossiness in them, which told me quite a lot. He had a moment of silent crying, then he shook his head.

I feel sad, for what is happening between me and my daughter he said.

It took him a while to calm down after talking to his haughtier. I find it hard just knowing what Sio is going through with his daughter, and the more we spoke, the more he found it difficult to come to terms with all that was taking place in his life.

From a father's point of view, as difficult as it is, for him to deal with the problems at hand he seems to put up a severe resistance, to the changes, when he should enjoy his retirement, since working hard to achieve what he owned.

At least, he had a legitimate point for all the turmoil in his life at present, because of the treatment his daughter has done to him, and duping him into moving into an elderly home. Sio has all his faculties intact, although he said to me once that sometimes he forgets things, but not all the time. The things he has difficulties with are his hygiene, nothing and preparing meals.

My boy he said, at my house I had someone that came cook, and took me for groceries, and any appointments that I had to go to.

How does it make you feel not being able to go anywhere?

Very frustrating he said, when I think about my house. I asked myself, when am I going to get out of this home, and get back to my house in the city? Instead of living in a place where I have no friends, and can't talk to anyone that is passing in front the home.

That my friend, I cannot give you an answer, because I am not in charge of you I replied.

I am so upset with my daughter right now and I don't want her around me, or ever want her to call me he said.

Do you want your tea, at the usual time Margaret said?

No! he answered back. Just put it in a thermos, and leave it on the table inside. I will take it when I am ready.

Margaret he said, I am sorry for yelling at you, in my angry tone of voice.

Sio, do you think your daughter has your best interest, looking after you?

My boy, he said to tell you the truth; I don't even know?

The reason for asking is, I know your daughter is the only one of your children that is living on the island, and your other children are living abroad.

I think so, he said, but the way she went about the whole situation duping me to live here, which I did not really want, gets me angry every time, just thinking about the way she used me to get the house renovated is heart wrenching.

Do you think you could have lived in the house while it was being renovated?

Maybe and maybe not, he said. She may have thought with all the construction that I would be in the way of the workers.

You may have a point there I said.

Yes! But it was my house, and it was all her doing, without me having anything to say or give my opinion about the situation.

A point well taken, I said, but it could have been a reason that was needed to be made with no delaying.

Would you have tried to stall getting the house renovated? I asked?

At this point, my boy, thinking where I am now, to what I have in the city, I would have to say yes!

I am sure she meant well, but you will have to talk to her calmly if you want to get back to see your home after they have completed it.

I will not make any promise he said, but I will try my best. Excuse me for a bit. I need to get my tea.

Ah! He said, this is a good cup of tea.

Is that so I replied.

Yes! My boy, that's a perfect cup of tea, he said.

He rests the cup of tea on the table, and stood up, looking towards the end of the driveway, as the people passed by, waving and shouting to them. After having a late tea break, and relaxing, it was not long before it would be time for supper, and there after Margaret leave for her home.

James takes over where Margaret left off, doing the nightly routines before retiring for the night. You can tell when Sio enjoyed his supper because he cleans his plate and let you know it was good.

Now! That was a delicious supper tonight. Margaret outdid herself today, he said.

I am glad you enjoyed every bit of it, unlike two days ago when you did not eat much, I said.

He said good night to me and thanked Margaret for the delicious supper.

You are welcome, Margaret said to him.

Sio got up from the chair, and made his way from the verandah walking carefully through the living room, making no contact with James, who was sitting on the couch, not even as much as goodnight to him, and entered his room slamming the door behind him.

I made my way down the steps after telling James goodnight, and he did the same. I took a shower and relaxed while listening to music. I had on my mp3 player, thinking about what Sio said to me today before falling asleep. Although the night was warm, the breeze was a little cooler coming off the ocean.

The morning came quickly, awakened by the neighbor's rooster that kept crowing constantly, as though it was right under the window of my bedroom. It was five am when I looked and with all that noise; it was hard returning to sleep again.

At this time of the morning, it was getting brighter, and a walk was in order. I got ready for a pleasant morning walk, enjoying the fresh air and the cool breeze. It was another hour and a half before I return to the house, and sitting on the verandah was Sio.

Good morning my boy, he said, is there any mangoes I can get if you can find them, and can you pick the papaw on the tree? I would like to have it before breakfast, please.

Good morning to you too I replied, back to him.

How many mangoes are they, and how many papaws he asked?

About six mangoes today, and I have two papaws. How many mangoes do you want today I asked?

Maybe two mangoes, and one of the papaw he said.

Here are the mangoes, and the papaw I replied.

Thank you kindly, my boy, was his response.

After handing him the fruits, I returned to my room, took a shower, and had my breakfast a couple of eggs and toast before returning upstairs to see what Sio was up to. On my arrival, he was busy eating the mangoes with a big smile on his face.

Sio was simply not ready for breakfast; but continued sucking the mangoes, and after he finished, the mangoes started on the papaw, with the juice of the mangoes still on the side of his lips and fingers.

Sio looks so happy when eating any fruits, putting aside any problems he is facing for the time. His face says it all, his eyes wide open, a smile on his face, makes me think he is not thinking about any animosity towards his daughter or James for taking him away from his home that he built.

Margaret, he shouted, can I get two slices of toast, with peanut butter, and a cup of tea, please?

Okay, Margaret replied. I will bring it up shortly.

Um! That was good, thank you God, he said.

Let's talk about religion and faith I said. Do you believe in God?

Do you believe in God he asked?

Yes! I do? I replied.

My boy, within the context of my faith, I once believed, but once in a while I have doubts. It is sometimes off and on, and I wish it could be better, he said.

Why? Do you say you wish it could be better I asked?

Well, my boy, part of my failure is not attending church, and not praying, giving thanks once in a while to my maker, he said.

What is stopping you from attending church I asked?

There is a church opposite the entrance, and I wish I could attend. Because of my outburst, I am not allowed. I wish someone can take me sometime he said.

The days seem to go by so fast and, now that evening is winding down, the sun was dipping lower and lower behind the coconut, and mango trees, giving way to the darkness of the night, the night creatures was making their nightly music for all to hear and the fireflies was blinking as the fly.

Good night my boy he said.

Good night and thank you for the talk, and your time today I replied.

I headed down the steps, and entered the downstairs living room, and straight to my room after my nightly routine relaxed for a while, giving thanks to God for another day before going to sleep for the night. The crowing rooster of the neighbors woke me up at the crack of dawn.

I got dressed after my morning routine and headed out for my morning walk. I took a different route, ended up walking longer than I had intended. It was a good and invigorating walk, met some people walking along the way, talked for a while, paying no attention to the sun and how hot it was getting.

The couple of people I was walking with reached their destination, and I had another half mile to walk before reaching the entrance of the driveway, looking towards the verandah sat Sio; waiting for me in a good mood.

He shouted, good morning.

I waved to him, saying good morning.

How was your walk, and how far did you walk this time?

My walk was great, and I only walked for about four miles, I said.

That's great my boy; is there any mangoes under the tree this morning he asked?

Let me see if there are any, yes; there are about six that I can find.

That's great, can I have a few, I mean about three he replied?

You sure can, I said.

Thank you, thank you, I will wait for a while before eating them he said.

I am going to have a shower, and my breakfast, then I will be back to talk to you.

Ok! My boy, he replied.

On my way up to see Sio, I had a brief conversation with James, lasting around twenty minutes.... he left soon after our conversation for a nearby town which was about fifteen minutes away. I finally went up to see Sio. He was still in a great mood. His face shaved and had a smile stretching from ear to ear. As he kept watching the mangoes, then his eyes glanced towards the papaw tree.

My boy; there are two half-ripe ones, do you think I can have them; both he asked?

You sure can. I don't see why not I replied?

Thank you for helping me all the time he said.

No problems, I will help you the best way possible I answered back.

What do you think rain with that dark cloud forming in the island's southeast he asked?

I think so. Dark clouds mean rain from the way it looks I said.

Sio, Margaret called to him, are you ready for your breakfast?

Oh, yes, please! Was his response.

When his breakfast brought to him, he looked at it, rubbing his hands together. He smiled.

Yummy! This looks good this morning.

Margaret! I am all done with breakfast.

Okay, she replied, I will be out to get the dishes shortly.

Let's talk a little about your childhood while growing up on the island with your mother and grandmother.

Okay, I did not really know my father. He was working on another island, and sent money home for us.

How often did you see your father?

Not much, maybe twice a year or whenever he can.

What was your father like?

I remember him being a tall man, very muscular, had black hair, brown eyes, and a brown complexion.

Were you close to dad? I asked.

Not really; but I respected him for what he was doing for my mother and me.

My father was a hard worker. When he died, I was about thirteen years of age. It hurt my mother, and she cried every day for a month.

Did things return to normal, after your mother stopped crying.

Yes! It did. She began gaining her composure. Then things began returning slowly back to normal as possible.

Was it hard at first for your mother?

For sure! They were some difficulties, once in a while.

My mother was short, stood about five feet six inches, long straight brown hair, and had a stride that drove men wild, he said.

How old was your mom when she met your father?

She was in her late twenties, but belonged to my dad.

How about your grandmother?

My grandmother was in her late sixties, and had a way about her that you would have loved. She was about two inches taller than my mother.

A bit on the heavy side, long black hair, brown eyes, and a light brow in complexion.

Did your grandmother, gave you any advice while you were growing up?

Oh yes! She would always say to me, son, listen to your mother, always try to obey her, and you will turn out alright.

Did you do what your grandmother told you?

Yes! I did whatever she told me? Was his response?

One day, after school, I came home and saw many people on the verandah, and the yard of the house, He said.

What happened? Why were so many people at the house?

I was around ten years old. I did not know what to make of it?

What did you do?

I approached the steps, my mother came out, gave me a hug, told me that my grandmother died in her sleep while taking a nap.

What did you make of it at the time?

I did not think she was dead. I thought she was sleeping. I kept hugging my mother, crying, but no tears trickled down my cheeks.

After; you had stopped hugging your mother, and crying, what did you do?

I walked into the house, and went to the bedroom, my grandmother was laying on the bed, dressed; in white, her favorite church outfit.

Did you believe, that your grandmother was dead at that moment?

At that moment; when I saw her with in her white dress, I will have to say yes; this time she was not walking to church, but would be driven to church in style; while the people attending the funeral service, had to walk behind the Hearst.

Were you now able to accept the fact, your grandmother would not be around anymore?

You see, my boy, at that moment, I had to face reality, and realize that life goes on.

How soon after your grandmother's death was she buried?

Let me explain, in the village where I grew up, it was customary for the burial of the deceased to be done quickly, that is within a day after death.

Why so soon, I asked?

The reason was, they were no place in the village to take the body to be kept; what we know today as embalming, he said.

Were there any rituals that took place before the burial?

Yes! There was, the carpenter in the village usually made the coffin out of any kind of wood he had available. A wake took place before and after the burial.

What did the wake comprise, if I may ask?

Sure, he said, it was a time to remember the dead, praying for their soul, for a safe passage to heaven.

Did anything else took place after the funeral service and burial?

Yep! After the burial, people in the village and those that knew my grandmother came over to the house, bringing food and drinks, mostly talking about my grandmother, how she was a wonderful person, always willing to help wherever she could.

How did you cope with death?

The best way I could, by keeping busy, as the days, weeks and months passed.

Were you okay, after those months had passed?

Yes! Sure was he said; I remember the day when I finished school, and was about to look for a job, so; I can have some money in my pocket and help my mother.

What happened? Did you find a job right away?

No! not at first. Job hunting took me a while, but I got one eventually in a small factory.

Were you happy that you found a job at the time?

Yes, I was; three years after the death of my grandmother, I dreamt she was sitting at the foot of my bed, one night; before falling asleep.

Were you scared?

Sure, won't you; I called out to my mother, and she asked what was wrong?

What did your mother say to you; when you told her what you saw?

It's nothing to be afraid of, he said. "she was only here to say her goodbye" and to make sure things were alright with you.

After Sio had finished telling me what happened, the night he saw his grandmother, the sky opened up, and the rain came down heavily. The wind became stronger, in the distance, especially, the coconut trees were swaying back and forth.

The wind blew the rain onto the verandah and had to evacuate the area where we sat. Sio went to his room, and I to mine, during that time I had a nap, until the rain subsided.

The sun came out hotter than before. Looking at the rooftops, you could see the vapor rising. As the sun beat down on the wet roof, that were mostly built of metal.

I heard a faint voice calling my name, much to my surprise. Are you coming upstairs for a visit before the night sets in he asked?

Sure! I said, but it would be in twenty minutes, give and take.

That's okay with me, he replied.

Is that what I think you are eating?

Yes, it is. I am having crackers, cheese, and a cup of tea. Hold on; while I answer the phone he said.

Okay, I will wait till you have finished speaking.

He said, "hello"

That was my cue to leave him for a while, with a big smile on his face.

Hello! My boy, are you coming back up he asked?

Just for a while I said.

Why are you smiling and laughing at I asked?

Well! My boy, I had a friendly conversation with my girlfriend, that lives in Canada. She wanted to know how I was doing, and that she still loves me. He said.

That's good to hear, then you had a good time talking; because I heard you laughing I said.

Yes! My boy, it was a good conversation, as always. Let's change the subject for a while.

Okay; what would you like to talk about?

What I want to know is why am I still living at the home?

Sio, this is what James told me, your house needs some major repairs, and some materials were not available at the hardware store, pushing back the completion date.

I am tired of being here. Good night, he said, that's it for now.

Good night, I replied.

I returned to my room, relaxed reading, and listening to music, before retiring for the night; with the sound of the night creatures and their mating songs. It was hard falling asleep. After listening to the sounds for a while, they became soothing to the mind.

At day break, I remained in bed for a little longer, relaxing and reading the newspaper, before visiting Sio, later in the day.

Sio, what happens to you, why are you looking so gloomy?

My daughter called. The moment I heard her voice things changed, he said.

Sio's temperament changed so rapidly, as though someone opened a faucet, letting the water flow through the hose, gushing out with a force of pure anger.

It's not that I was listening to his conversation, I was within hearing distance. I heard him swearing and calling his daughter's names. I have never heard him use before, much to my surprise, never knew he had such a vocabulary of words in his arsenal.

My boy, he said. My daughter works in the American Consulate office as a secretary, educated in England and moved to the island.

Is she married? I asked?

Yes, she is. But I have her husband. "Oh God" what have I done to deserve to live in this home when I already have my home.

Do you remember what you told me a week ago about visiting the home, and you told your daughter you can live here?

Yes, but; I was never planning to do that so soon; you mean all that talk at the time got me here?

Yes! I replied. It sure did.

After we both said our good night, I went to my room, fell asleep for a short time. I woke up, walked to the front entrance of the downstairs living room, looked eastward, the moon was just rising over the horizon.

The sky was clear, looking up at the stars that shone brightly with no restrictions from the clouds. It was very peaceful watching the moon rise, the stars in the sky without a sense of urgency.

I sat on the wall at the side of the home, looking at the brilliant scene of the moon rising in the sky. It's reflection of the moon over the ocean was a lit path straight towards the home, as though anyone could get up and walk on the water towards the moon.

A boat's bow entered; the space that was made by the moon's path. The scene was very captivating, making it the perfect picture for a postcard. I returned to my room shortly thereafter; and slept till daybreak.

My days were getting shorter, as my vacation was ending for the time I had to spend on the island before returning to Canada. In our conversation, promised Sio, I would return the following year to visit him, and see if they were any changes he had made about his daughter.

Sio, please! Promise me you will try your best to get along with your daughter.

Okay my boy, I will try my best to be polite to her, and not call her names, he said.

Remember; she is your flesh and blood, and no one wants to be treated in the manner you are exercising.

Sio, I will be going into town; they are somethings, I need to take care about.

Okay; what time would you be back, he asked?

I hope to be back, before it gets dark, around five thirty, I said.

I walked down to the entrance of the drive way, looking back, Sio watched me get into a mini-bus heading towards town.

I returned later than expected. Around six thirty (6:30) pm, Sio was sitting outside on the verandah, taking in the cool breeze, blowing off the ocean.

"Hello my good man he shouted,"

Hi, I replied.

How was your trip into town?

It was very eventful, I responded.

I said good night to Sio, went to my room, took a shower, and changed into my night attire. I slept until morning. The sun was already raising the heat for the day.

After my morning rituals, made my way upstairs to visit Sio, he was already sitting on the verandah, finished his breakfast, all dressed to my surprise.

Sio, try to understand what I am about to tell you, not that your daughter does not want to talk with you I said.

Then; what is it he asked?

You need to have a pleasant conversation with her, instead of swearing at her, every time she calls to talk with you?

She makes me angry, because of what she did to me. I cannot let it go, he replied.

I know she may be tired with the way you are treating her. It does not mean that she does not love you I said.

Then why? Do I always get angry, just hearing her voice? He replied.

She did all this because she wants what is best for you. She thinks you will abuse her every time she calls to talk to you.

His facial expression said a lot and it may have disturbed him, giving him something to think about. He closed his eyes for a moment, as the tears rolled down his cheeks. He wiped the tears, opened his eyes, smiled, nodded his head, as if to say, yes! I got what you are saying to me.

I would like my daughter to treat me with respect. He said.

Yes! I replied, I think she respects you, but you must realize, you are in this home, because you could not look after yourself.

I know, all I thinking is she wanted the house for herself, he said.

So; what do you think, now that you know, she does not want your house?

Looking up to the sky; said "thank you for talking to me, and allowing me to vent my frustrations out on you."

I am glad we had these conversations, so; you can realize what your daughter is doing for you... okay.

Silence for a while...... Margaret, I am ready for my tea, with two slices of toast and peanut butter please.

Looking towards the ocean, said if I was younger, and had mobility, I would go walking along the rocks on the beach looking for whelks.

You would! I replied.

Do you know what whelks are?

Sure! "I told him" it's something like conch, that holds on to rocks, and has to be pried then off.

Good! You know about whelks.

Putting the cup of tea to his lips said "wow" that's excellent tea.

I gave him a chance to have his tea and toast. We began talking for a bit after he had finished. The street lights came on just as dusk was settling in and the night take over.

Good night, he said.

Good night, I replied.

We went to our separate rooms, showered, and did my night hygiene, changed into nightclothes, laid on the bed thinking, in a couple days I would leave the island, heading for another island, spending some time, with my best friend since; childhood before returning to Canada.

In fact, I could not fall asleep right away, they were scenes playing out in my mind, and finally fell asleep with no further distractions. I got up early next morning changed into my walking attire, and was off for a long walk.

I walked for three hours before returning to the home. Sio was sitting on the verandah, watching me as I walk up the driveway. I could see his head, just a tad above the railing where he was sitting.

He waited until I got close enough to say; "good morning" are you coming up for a visit?

Yes! After I had a shower, and had my breakfast.

Good! He said, then we can talk for a bit before you start anything today.

Margaret, he shouted. I am ready for my shower and morning hygiene.

Okay! She said, I will be there shortly.

Any other time, he would say he was ready to have his shower, but dance around for a long time before taking his shower. This time he was the one initializing it. Sio was serious, and as promised, had his shower and morning hygiene, before his breakfast and our conversation.

Sio knew my time was getting shorter as the days went by, so; Sio wasted no time wanting to get a lot off his mind before I left the island.

My boy! I had a dream that I set the home on fire, and was now able to get away from here and return to my house.

Am I hearing from you correctly, I said.

Yes! He replied.

As soon as he had said those words, James was walking by, and Sio literally yelled and accused him of having an affair with his daughter, which he thinks started a couple months ago, long before he came to the home.

Sio, went on with his shouting campaign, threatened to set fire to the home, just after he said to me; he had a dream of carrying out the act. He has shown the hatred he has towards James.

Are you calm enough, so; we can continue our conversation I asked?

I don't think so; right now, "I feel like killing James."

Why is that?

For everything he has done to me.

What has James done to you? He deserves your abuses.

He agreeing with my daughter, getting me out of the house I built, bringing me here to the home in the countryside, which is a piece of junk.

Sio, in the morning I will leave very early for the city, and returning late in the evening.

My boy, that will be okay with me, and went inside.

The next morning, I got up before the neighbor's rooster started crowing. I got dressed, walked out the door, and waited for the mini-bus to the city of St. Georges to conduct some business. But the city does not come alive until 9:15 am, giving me enough time to sit and have a

As I looked out the window, I appreciated the greenery, the amazing landscape of buildings along the hillside, and the color schemes that popped amongst the trees, only seen on the Caribbean islands.

I spent some time in the small town, after arriving from the city, entered the internet café, to check my emails and bank account balance. I made friends with the people there had a substantial breakfast, comprising two eggs, fried plantain toast, and cocoa tea.

Towards the east sun was already up over the mountains. The temperature rose, making it hot and uncomfortable, but it is something the people live with throughout the year. I had to get accustom with for the next couple days before my holidays were over, and can leave the island.

My focus today is getting my affairs done fast as possible, return to the countryside, where it is much cooler. As the day progressed, so; did the heat, and hardly any breeze blowing to cool you down. As I walk, I can see the beads of perspiration running down the faces of the people passing by.

I got all my affairs completed within two and a half hours. I wanted to stay a little longer, but got back to the countryside where it was much cooler. My drive from the city to the countryside took a little more that forty-five minutes. The mini-bus had to be filled with passengers before the driver left the bus depot.

As the bus driver drove through the mountains, around bends, and curves, it was quite an experience. Breath-taking vistas, and the greenery of the vegetation along the side of the road, was something to be enjoyed.

I had supper before catching a mini-bus home.

I got off the bus; I heard a familiar voice shouting out to me. It was the voice of Sio. He could not wait for me to get closer. Walking up the incline, Prince the dog barked for the first time since being there almost a month.

My boy, are you coming up for a visit he asked?

Yes! I will come for a quick visit, I replied.

I just want to see a familiar face, instead of James's, whom I hate, with a passion. I wish I could eradicate him.

That is not the way to talk. James is the one who has provided a roof over your head.

I know that, my boy. I still wish I could eradicate him.

Sio, you are all talk you know down in your heart; you cannot carry out any threats on James. remember he was a police officer.

Are we going to talk tomorrow again he asked?

Yes! We are. I will spend some time with you before I leave. Is that okay I said?

My boy: that will be great he replied.

Good night I said, walked down the steps to my room, took a shower, laid on the bed, started thinking, because I had not finished my conversations with him. The morning came quickly as the night, slept longer because of the hectic day before, giving me time to recuperate. I could hear Sio calling my name as I washed my face.

Sio, Margaret said, he is not awake yet; you know he will come and see you when he is ready.

I walked up the steps into the verandah. Sio had a smile on his face never seen before. All the time I was there. It was the happiest I have seen for a while.

Good morning my boy, he said, how did you sleep last night?

Great! I replied.

With a sinister smile, looked at me, what are you doing today?

Not much, just going to relax, do some packing I replied.

"I guess it's that time for you to leave soon."

Yes! "I said" It was nice knowing you, and everything you shared with me.

No problems! He said it was a pleasure talking with you.

Thank you for letting me write about our conversations.

My boy! "knowledge is power. The more you know, the better,"

Sio, how do you feel about the situation we have been discussing.

The truth, good! I know it's hard work. I have to try working things out with my daughter, instead of calling her every name I can find.

Good, I am going to miss you very much. We had some wonderful conversations amongst ourselves.

Yes! We sure did. No one will sit and talk to me the way you did, especially listening to what I had to say.

Is there anything else you would like to say?

The whole matter was being placed at the home in the countryside. I was away from everything, also everyone I knew. I was saying this especially placing me here *AGAINST MY WISHES*, more so; by my daughter and James.

A point well taken, but; your house needed major repairs, from what James told me, was all your daughter's decision.

It's not that I am against having the repairs done in the house. It is the way she went about it that makes me angry with her.

Yes! Given the situation, it was on the spur of the moment. The workmen had a time they had given her, so; the work could begin and finished on time.

But; "I did not have to move out of the house." While the work was being done.

I will have to disagree with you, you will have been in the way of everyone, telling them how to do their job. It is the reason your daughter place you at the home.

My boy, I don't believe that. And l never would have disturbed the workers one iota, but; I may want to help.

I don't think your daughter would leave you here at the home, for the rest of your life knowing how miserable you feel being here.

Why do you say that he asked?

I think she knows her father well enough.

I am going to promise you, no matter the outcome. All I can say is will do my best to get along with everybody, that has my best interest.

I think your daughter is doing the best she can to make you comfortable. I don't think she is going to take you for a ride or should I say con you out of anything.

I also think you need give her credit, and stop discrediting he, behind her back.

Do you think, I am doing all those things to her?

Yes! Spreading rumors, telling people you talk to, what your daughter is doing to you, which in fact not true, when viewed from her eyes.

Man! That's heavy he replied.

I do not think for a minute; your daughter wants your house. She has one of her own.

My boy! I know it's getting late; can we talk just a little more?

Sure! We can, what do you want to talk about?

Nothing really, just sitting around, enjoying your company is good enough he said.

You know, that it's getting late, so; let's say our goodnight.

Good night my boy, see you in the morning, before you leave.

Okay; I will make sure I come, and see you before leaving.

Margaret was in the kitchen, doing some last minute chores, Sio is a good hearted man, but can be very difficult at times to work with she said.

What do you make of it now, do you see any change in him?

He is much better since you are having conversations with him.

Thank you, have a good night, safe journey home, and I will see you in the morning.

I went to my room, did some more packing, because I was departing from the countryside home and Sio. It has been a very good month at the home, met Sio, and listened to many of his conversations.

It was late, before I completed packing, made sure everything was in my suitcase, took a shower changed, resting my head on the pillow, hoping to fall asleep, but it did not happen quickly. I was thinking about my flight, Sio's demeanor after leaving, would he revert to his old habits? Or; continue to co-operate with Margaret.

I awoke early, before the rooster crowed, went for a quick walk. My last in this part of the countryside, passed and bye to people I met, and got to know. I returned after an hour and a half, showered, changed into clean clothes, had breakfast, before going upstairs to have a last conversation with Sio. They were tears running down his cheeks, as; I approached him; he did not have to say a word. I knew exactly how he felt at that moment.

"I am going to miss you my boy." He said.

Same here, I replied.

What time are you leaving for the airport he asked?

I one hour time, after we chat for a bit, is that okay with you?

It sure is; okay with me he said.

Time .... flew by fast.

I am going promise to call you from time to time.

Okay; he said.

Good bye Sio, it was nice meeting, and knowing you, promise me you will not give trouble to anyone, especially Margaret.

I promise that I will not, he said.

James, although we had little time to talk, thank you for having me at the home.

It was great having you here. Anytime you want to return, drop me an email.

I will gladly do that; you will surely hear from me. I replied.

I collected my suitcase and backpack, strolled down the driveway to the end of the entrance. Looking back, Sio was waving and shouting.

Have a pleasant trip, and a safe one.

A regular mini-bus driver, I travelled with stopped for me, and I was on my way to the airport. I kept thinking of Sio, all the way to the airport, what he might think? And what he might do if provoked? It played on my mind like a re-occurring decimal. Suddenly no more thoughts of him.

I cleared customs, had an hour to spare, did some shopping at the duty-free shop, purchased some alcohol for some friends in Trinidad next stop for the next three months.

Finally; that familiar word everyone was waiting to hear. All passengers on flight 741 are now boarding. Gathering my backpack, duty-free items, proceeded to the gate where I had to show my boarding pass and passport. At the plane entrance, the hostess pointed me to where I was going to be seated. After securing my luggage in the overhead compartment, I sat and fastened my seatbelt.

I landed in Trinidad half hour after taking off. My friend greeted me at the exit door of the airport and was on my way to his home on a farm. I spent another three months helping him with chores that needed taking care of, and also relaxing when the temperatures was too hot to work. The months flew by quickly and was glad to leave the heat and return home.

The flight took approximately five hours and forty minutes after taking off from Trinidad. It felt good to be home, arriving in time for the spring weather, other than the heat in the sunny islands. My daughter arrived just as I was exiting the terminal, met me at the destination point, I gave her, and had lunch before driving me home.

It has been a month since; returning from my four months' vacation. I made a couple of calls to Sio, but he could not remember me.

Hello! Sio, it's me, I said.

Who are you he replied?

Don't you remember me, from a couple months back?

No! he replied.

Well, let me jog your memory. People call you the money man, and you worked at Heinz in England.

Ah! Yes, my boy. How are you?

I am good; how are you and your daughter getting along?

Well! My boy, to tell you the truth, we had words a couple of times.

Was it bad, as before, or was it worst?

Let's not talk about it, he said.

Behave yourself, I said.

Goodbye; .... silence.

I took longer between calls to Sio. This time he wanted to talk about the way his daughter treated him, and did not see the way he was treating her. What daughter under this circumstance would want to be treated by a father in a hostile way.

I made two calls, after my initial call, and had a normal conversation with him.

Sio, if you show her respect, no more insults, towards her, things would have been different by now.

My boy; although I am angry with her, most of the time, I still love her.

I can tell that you do; a father would always love his daughter, no matter what, after all, it's your flesh and blood.

Thanks my boy, good talking to you. Goodbye now.

Goodbye, I will call you soon.

I continued to keep in touch with Sio, once every two weeks, actually to find out how he was doing, but most of the time, he was always angry at his daughter, except on one occasion.

Sio, how are you doing today?

I am okay, and doing much better.

You sound happy, "why are you so elated,"

My boy; for the first time, "I spoke to my daughter, without calling her any names."

How does it make you feel?

Great; I hope it can continue, he said.

Do your best. Do not pick any arguments with her?

My boy! I will try to curb my anger whenever; I talk to her.

If you continue, maybe; she would reconsider and forgive you all the wrong things you said to her.

I am hoping so; my boy, I am hoping so;

You will have to first apologize to her. And hope this moment you are having with your daughter last.

Me! Apologize, do I have to?

Yes! For her to see that you are trying to change, and talk to her politely. It is a good start.

Okay! My boy, he said.

Goodbye, I will call you in two weeks?

The weeks went by, as promised, I made the call.

Hello! Is Sio there, can I speak to him, tell him it's Tom?

He is not in; this is Margaret; James took him out for a drive.

Is he behaving as promised?

Yes! We have noticed big changes in his behavior. James asked him if he would like to go out.

What did he say?

Yes! She said, and James said okay, and they left about an hour ago.

Thanks for the update Margaret, tell Sio that I will call him again in two weeks. Have a good day. Bye!

Sio, how are you doing these days?

Great! Went out with James. He took me to the seashore for a swim.

Good to hear that you are doing great.

My boy! I am still focused on returning; to my home, where I belong.

I quite understand that, but give it more time. With the changes you have made, it will just be a matter of time.

My boy! My daughter wants me to stay at the home, where I can get proper care around the clock. I agree with the proper care, but I had someone looking after me daily at my house.

You told me this already, what is wrong with staying at the home?

Simple; I cannot go where I dammed well pleased. Here I am restricted. If my behavior was good, James takes me out when time permitted.

Well! inappropriate behavior does not warrant being taken out, do you agree?

Good bye... Silence.

I know, I left Sio with something to think about. Implementing changes in his behavior is another topic he has to deal with. I kept in touch with him for most of the year and called him for Christmas.

Hello! This time, James answered the phone.

How are you doing?

Great, and you Tom, how is everything with you?

Good as well; how is Sio doing? Is he there?

No! his daughter finally had enough of him, planned to get him home, where he always wanted to be from the first day.

Ok, I will see you in a couple months.

Okay, take care will talk later.

Yes! We will talk again soon.

I returned to the home one year later, to see James; but did not stay at the home. I spent only two weeks on the island, but stayed with my aunt,

Margaret said to me, before leaving, Sio asked about kerosene and matches, so; he could burn the home to the ground, so that no one else could stay there. He thought it was a horrible place. Before leaving, James gave me Sio's phone number.

Hello! I said.

Hello! The voice replied.

Sio this is Tom; do you remember me?

Not really; should I know you?

Yes! Do you remember our conversations a year ago at the home in the countryside? You told me about your daughter, where you lived, and where you worked in England.

Yes! Yes! Is that you, my boy?

It sure is; now you remember.

Yes! Where are you now?

On the island, I was thinking of visiting you. Are you going to be home tomorrow around 10:30 in the morning?

Yes! I will, don't have any place to go.

Okay! I will see you tomorrow.

Good my boy, looking forward to seeing you, goodbye.

I went to see Sio the following day as planned, had to walk to the top of a hill, where the golf course was located, suddenly I heard a voice calling to a chap, that was passing, and I knew that was the voice I am familiar with.

When he saw me, his face lit up, my boy! It's good to see you.

Good to see you too; how have you being keeping?

Good! I had a new caregiver, had to fire her, she was not taking me serious.

What made you fire her? Was it something she was not doing?

Yes! She wanted to do things her way, and was not doing things how I wanted it done. Let's just say she was not complying with anything I told her.

Who is looking after you now?

I got my old caregiver back, the one I had before moving to the home in the countryside.

What is her name?

Miss Lynette; let me introduce you to her, Miss Lynette. Can you come for a minute, please.

Yes, I can, the voice echoed back.

Miss Lynette, let me introduce you to Tom. We met at the home in the countryside where I stayed.

Please to meet you, I am sure you have your hands full.

Yes! Sometimes I do, but not all the time.

Miss Lynette was short, long straight hair, smooth skin, and a very light skin tone.

Do you get along with her, without giving problems?

Yes, we do. She understands me, prepares all my meals for the day, and leaves me by myself in the evening, until next morning.

Why is that? Does she not sleep at the house?

No, that is the arrangements we agreed on.

I understand from James, you called, asking if he was coming to take you back to the home.

Yes, I called, and asked. His answer was an emphatic no!

Sio, I am amazed at the view you have in the front of your house.

Are you; then take a look at the backyard.

I will, but right now, how are you doing?

Miss Lynette, can you bring my walking stick please, so; I can chase these birds.

I told you, stop feeding them, and they will stop coming Miss Lynette said.

Okay; I will stop?

I excuse myself for a while, had a talk with Miss Lynette. How is he really doing?

He is difficult very stubborn, at bathing time, at his regular schedule, she said.

It was the same at the home, do not take it too seriously. He will ask when he wants it.

Did his daughter ever call him, since; he came back?

Yes! Once a week to see if he was okay, but does not visit because of his attitude towards her.

I returned to the verandah after talking to Miss Lynette.

Sio, do you remember all the things we talked about at the home?

Vaguely! Let's move on to other things.

Okay! Do you appreciate the effort your daughter put into getting the house renovated?

Yes! I do; but I have to get accustomed to the new and improve things that were done to the house.

Sio, are you telling me you approve all of it.

Yes! "You can say that."

Question? How is your relationship with your daughter?

Not good, please; change the subject, don't want to talk about my daughter?

What; do you want to talk about?

My boy, what brought you here to see me? I am glad to see you.

I came to see how you are doing, since; you made a good impression on me.

Okay, good enough for me. Let me take you on a tour of the house, since they renovated it.

Okay, let's do just that. Why the grin on your face?

I am just happy to see you my boy.

The house looked wonderful, with all the comfort you will ever need.

Yes! It has more than I will ever use, anyway.

After the tour we made our way back on the verandah, and enjoyed the view, looking towards the golf course. The sound of people's voices came riding in the air to the sound of music to Sio's ear.

Hello, there have a good day! he shouted as the passed in front his house.

Please excuse me for a moment. I will be right back.

Sure! Take your time.

I went into the kitchen, had a chat with Miss Lynette, and asked her how was Sio, doing?

Miss Lynette, how is Sio doing really?

He has his moments. He was talking about burning down the house.

Seriously!

Yes! So; I had to remove all matches, and paper out of sight, where they cannot be found, as; a precaution for his own safety.

Really! Thanks for the information.

Sio's mind wanders at times. It's not that he has Alzheimer's, he does. not, he just simple would not talk about anything that is not relevant to him simple put. He called out to his caregiver to bring him his walking stick. That very moment a vendor was passing in front his house.

Hello! He shouted, what is the price of your oil?

The vendor replied, eight dollar's sir, do you need a bottle?

No thanks, not today.

My boy, you know that I just came back from England three years ago?

Yes! That's what you told me last year; when we talked at the home.

I remember the days at the home. I could see you from the verandah when you left for your walks up the road.

Did I ever mentioned to you why I was going up the road?

Not really, maybe you did at some point.

Sio, the front exterior of the house looks small, but looks can be deceiving.

Yes, but when you get inside, you see the difference in size.

Are you satisfied with the complete renovations your daughter got done to the house?

Yes! With a smile on his face.

Can I call you by your other nickname, Labelle, this once?

Sure; you can my boy.

I notice you have a garage; do you have a car?

No! he does not have one, Miss Lynette replied.

You really have a magnificent view of the golf course at the front. But the ocean view of the ocean in the backyard is very spectacular.

I think so; that is one of the reason I bought the land here, and built my house.

Let's talk about your daughter for a bit; how is she doing?

My boy, to tell you the truth I don't know and don't really care.... Popped his walking stick, started shooting it off like a machine gun pow, pow, pow.

Has she come to see you?

No! she is avoiding me.

Did you do anything for her to avoid you?

Silence....

Would you ever want to return at the home, in the countryside?

Laughing.... Frankly, no way not on my mother's dead body.

Who brought you back to your house?

I came by taxi.

Who made the decision that you could return? Did you howl and bitch?

Smiling.... My daughter wanted my house, that is why she had it renovated, but she has her own house, not too far from here.

People passing... hello, there good morning, right on right on he shouted.

Does anything or anyone bother you at night?

Yes! The young people, loud noise, after partying, on their way home.

How do you get to your doctors, bank appointments and groceries shopping?

I have a special taxi driver I call anytime I have to go anywhere. He will come and take me where ever I need to go.

Have you ever gone to the market in the city?

No; not since I came back to the island. How is the market in town?

It was renovated, and is much smaller, from the market I knew a couple of years ago.

My boy; when are you returning to Canada?

On Friday, I said.

Would you be coming back to the island again?

Yes! Hopefully next year, if all goes well.

Would you be staying in the countryside at the home?

No; just going to be visiting the home.

Sio, are you ready for your bath, Miss Lynette asked?

Yes; I sure am?

My boy; It gave me something I did not have before the renovations........ He giggled.

Do you like the renovations that were done?

Yes, I do, but they made some changes without my input.

Would you have preferred to leave the house the way you knew it?

Yes! There are changes I find difficult to accept, but I would have to live with, no matter if I rebel.

Make use; of what you have at present.

Are you telling me I have to compromise and use all the things that my daughter put in the house for me.

Yes! That is exactly what I am saying. Conform to the new way of things, and forget the old.

So; you are telling me that modernization has the house looking good.

Yes, I understand. That it was not up to the new building code. What you have now is up to that standard.

So; you are telling me it is, and I should accept the changes.

Yes! Make yourself comfortable, use what you have and do not give yourself worries about what you had before.

I guess there are no other choices, for me, but to give in to the changes.

What your daughter did here was making sure that everything was up to code, making your house a safer place for you to live.

I guess you are right, my boy.

I do not know how things were then, but if you have to sell this house, you will get a reasonable price for it.

They did the painting the right way. It was not done slap and dash like other painters do.

My boy, I am my own boss, do what I want, when I want, and how I want things to be done.

I must say; I do admire you for your strong will and tenacity, never giving up on what you wanted.

Thank you my boy, I may be stubborn but let me tell you this, my long-term memory is slowly fading.

There are some things I have to tell you, thanks; for sharing your story with me in our conversations about your difficult situation you have gone through, not only as a teenager, but as an elderly person.

I knew Sio, in a short time, and with the vast amount of knowledge he has, makes me wonder how he became so cantankerous towards people, especially his own daughter.

He once said to me "watch and learn" but first you have to understand what to look for, and learn from it. As far as learning from his vast knowledge, I took a liking to him, not at our initial meeting, but several days after, being in the countryside, and also visiting him at his home.

He reminded me about the things that were on his list he wished to do, but could not, because of his behavior towards James. He came to realize, while talking to himself, if he had not threatened James, he might have gone out often.

Sio always said he had a home where he was comfortable, and I came to understand why. It was all the excitement; he saw in front his house when people pass by. He reminded me of all the things he had accomplished over the years while working at A J Heinz in England, and would have it no other way.

You know my boy, the house I had in England, and my lover. It was stupid of me to let her out of my life.

Why do you say that? You were stupid?

Because I let a good woman out of my life I really cared for.

My boy; I have two grandsons, one lives in Canada, the other lives on the island not too far away.

Does the one who lives on the island, visits you?

No! I do not see him because of my daughter.

Is he old enough to come by himself to visit you?

Yes, it hurts me, because I do not get along with my daughter. My grandson is being used to punish me.

I took another look at the backyard. It had all the fruit trees he needed, which he planted after building his house. The view was breathtaking. In the distance you could see the ocean, and the ships coming into the harbor to berth, especially the cruise lines.

Sio's time was mostly on the verandah, watching the golfers and chasing the birds.

My boy! Frequently, I wanted to burn the house down he said.

You need to put that thought out of your mind.

I will try my best to not think of it.

Can I offer you any money for the house? You can live in it for free until you die, then I will occupy it; only then.

Silence... looked at me and smiled.

Let me ask you a serious question. Has your daughter ever come to see you?

No! she is avoiding me, as much as possible. I had not talked to her in a couple of weeks.

So; you talk to her?

Yes! sometimes when I want some KFC, I would ask her to get it for me.

You like KFC a lot?

Yes! I wish I could have a couple of pieces of chicken and fries.

You have your food prepared already. KFC are special occasion. Whenever we do groceries and banking, Miss Lynette said.

Sio has a tremendous vocabulary of words, and I am amaze by words he uses, and can tell you what it meant. He tries not to use too many words in his conversations.

My boy, I know I have asked you this question before, when are you leaving for Canada?

On Friday.

Not for another year (2014) in time for the food festival.

I have seen both sides of Sio, and they are both similar. It's the behavior of an individual that does not want to be controlled, or told what to do

Can I help you with anything now, that I am here before I leave?

Yes. I need someone to give me direction once in a while, to help me make smart decisions.

Ok, what about your daughter?

Her; ha! I don't think so; not with a big smile on his face.

I notice a mango tree at the entrance, while I was coming in the driveway.

Yes! It is; I get my mangoes from the tree when it is in season.

I enjoyed my conversations with him, and his vast knowledge he threw at me. It was a sad occasion when our conversation was being concluded.

My boy, I will be okay, and will look forward to another visit whenever you return to the island.

Sio; all the best. Please! Do your best to behave.

I will try, but it may be impossible.

Miss Lynette, it's been a pleasure meeting you take care.... bye.

Walking towards the entrance of the driveway, all I can hear was;

Goodbye! Take care my boy.

I walked to where I was staying, and could not help thinking about him. Would he change within a year? Will he remember me? The conversations we shared, or will he look at me as though I was a stranger?

The most difficult thing for him is trying to reconcile for the lost relationship he severed with his daughter, because of his anger towards her. I left the island two days later, after my visit with Sio, returned to Canada but made no contact with him. I had forgotten my phone chip on the island where I stayed.

The year flew by so fast. I returned to the island and visited Sio. It was a surprise; he did not recognize me at first, his eyes sight was fading, but not until I called him by his other name.

"That voice?" I know that voice?

Sure! You do, I said.

He got up as I approached him, gave me a great handshake.

How are you, my boy?

Great to see you. How is your health, and your relationship with your daughter?

He smiled, not good.

Have you called her anytime since I left?

Nope!

You said you would try.

I could not bring myself to call, I called once. We argued, swore at her, and tell her where to stick her head.

He was still adamant about what she had done to him a couple years ago, leaving him in the countryside at the elderly home. She put me there and was "Held Against My Wishes" which I despised.

Are you going to let your relationship with your daughter suffer?

My boy! I cannot come to terms with all the problems she caused me in the last couple of years. That is all I am going to say, on the matter.

I spent about two hours visiting, thank him for some of the many advice he gave me, wish him and Miss Lynette well, and drove away. I left a wounded man behind with his miseries, which he had to deal with. Not coming to terms with forgiving his daughter is something he will have to live with until he is ready to do, or die; sad to say, but it's true.

I have never met his daughter, and could not hear her side of the story, why she placed her dad in the home. He may be cantankerous as we all aged, we become miserable, out of sorts, and forgetful. This is just part of life.

A few years after we concluded our conversations he got sick, had to be rushed to the hospital. I understood that he and his daughter had started to fix their relationship, before getting sick. I also learned he was lying in bed one afternoon gasping for breath, when he was taken to the hospital.

He spent a week in the hospital, and asked to go home, where he was comfortable. His daughter accepted his wishes, and he returned to his home two days later. I learned after returning home, died three weeks after, at 96 years. His daughter was at his bedside.

After all the animosity he had for her, it took him all these t-years, but finally came to terms apologizing for his behavior towards her and his grandchildren. I wished he had done it sooner. They buried him not too far from his home.

His funeral attendance with family, friends and those that knew him. It was unfortunate that I did not know about his death until they buried him. The courage and tenacity of the man they called Simon "Sio" or by his other name, Labelle, was an inspiration to me.

In writing the conversations about a man I came to admire, who had spunk at his age, full of life, and was not afraid to tell you that. He was not to be taken lightly. My hat goes off to him. He will be missed greatly.

FAREWELL
   A man who was full of life with his spunkiness.
   Who enjoyed friendly conversations, laughter and jokes.
   I salute you my friend at your passing.
   Truly knowing they were peace and love around you.
   Those you loved throughout the years.
   May you, resting in the arms of God.
   Farewell, but not forgotten.
   The End.

About the Author

Father of two children, with three grandchildren, and a greatgrandson comes from a family consisting of three boys and four sisters.He interest are fishing, hiking,and walking. He resides in the City of Mississauga, Ontario Canada.

www.ingramcontent.com/pod-product-compliance
Lightning Source LLC
Chambersburg PA
CBHW052209150726
48002CB00003B/1147